Has Marriage for Love Failed?

For Patrice Champion, in companionship

Has Marriage for Love Failed?

Pascal Bruckner

Translated by Steven Rendall and Lisa Neal

polity

First published in French as *Le mariage d'amour a-t-il échoué* © Editions Grasset & Fasquelle, 2010

This English edition © Polity Press, 2013

Polity Press
65 Bridge Street
Cambridge CB2 1UR, UK

Polity Press
350 Main Street
Malden, MA 02148, USA

ISBN-13: 978-0-7456-6978-6

A catalogue record for this book is available from the British Library.

Typeset in 12.5 on 15 pt Adobe Garamond
by Servis Filmsetting Ltd, Stockport, Cheshire
Printed and bound in Great Britain by the MPG Printgroup

The publisher has used its best endeavours to ensure that the URLs for external websites referred to in this book are correct and active at the time of going to press. However, the publisher has no responsibility for the websites and can make no guarantee that a site will remain live or that the content is or will remain appropriate.

Every effort has been made to trace all copyright holders, but if any have been inadvertently overlooked the publisher will be pleased to include any necessary credits in any subsequent reprint or edition.

For further information on Polity, visit our website: www.politybooks.com

Contents

v

CONTENTS

I have always heard from my youth that in America it is possible to get a divorce for incompatibility of temper. In my childhood I always thought it was a joke; but I thought it even more of a joke when I discovered that it was true. If married people are to be divorced for incompatibility of temper, I cannot imagine why all married people are not divorced. Any man and any woman must have incompatible tempers; it is the definition of sex.

G. K. Chesterton, *The Illustrated London News*,
19 September 1908

Preface

In Erbil, the capital of Iraqi Kurdistan, a group of French volunteers made a documentary film in 2009 about an old man who lives not far from a public dump and earns his living by collecting plastic jugs and jerrycans. In the film, he tells his life story, which is punctuated, like that of his people, by all kinds of misfortunes. While he is going down the list of bad things that have happened to him, he suddenly straightens up and declares: 'My greatest success in life? I married for love and have two children born in love.' His wife confirms this. Immediately the audience bursts into applause and adores the film. Iraqi Kurdistan, although it is prosperous and peaceful compared to the rest of the country, adheres by custom to a clan system that compels young people to enter into marriages arranged by their families. Honour killings and induced suicides are the lot of girls suspected of frequenting boys of their own choice. If so many young Kurds take refuge in Europe or the United States, it is as much for reasons of individual autonomy as for economic reasons; they want to experience consensual unions, to marry the person they love and not be forced to marry someone else.[1]

A strange situation: at the very time when freedom to love is exercising its seductive power on some traditional societies – Muslim countries, India, China (even if in the latter two nations the lack of women, resulting from selective abortions, throws the matrimonial market out of kilter) –, and when gays and lesbians in our societies are demanding the right to marry, marriage is undergoing a crisis of legitimacy in the West. In its traditional form, it was accused of many sins: it was inegalitarian and despotic, objectified women, and led to adultery and prostitution.

1 I thank Hugues Dewavrin for this information. The documentary, entitled 'Daba, ville des bidons,' comes from Alterdoc, an audio-visual non-governmental organization, and was directed by Baudouin Koenig.

Few institutions have aroused so much sarcasm and so much anger. In the contemporary form of marriage by consent that won out after the Second World War, it created new scourges without putting an end to the old ones: neither prostitution nor infidelity disappeared, whereas the number of divorces increased exponentially, and more and more people remained single. The history of traditional marriage was characterized by resignation to the conjugal prison or the repulsion it inspired; today its history, in Europe at least, is characterized by disaffection with it. Over time, it has had many adversaries before finally becoming its own best enemy. Out of concern for harmony, the twentieth century emancipated hearts and bodies; the result was an increase in discord. What happened? Was the enchanted palace of reciprocal affection no more than a dilapidated hovel? How could love, which has never known any law (*Carmen*) be subjected to law, since it is fuelled by transgression?

The Catastrophe of the Wedding Night

In his novel *Une Vie* (*A Life*, 1883), Guy de Maupassant tells the story of a young woman of the minor Norman nobility, Jeanne, who falls in love with a local viscount, Julien. On their wedding night, her father, urged on by his wife, takes her aside and delivers an awkward speech about what awaits her:

> My darling, [. . .] I don't know what you know about life. There are mysteries that are carefully concealed from children, and especially a girl, who must remain pure in mind, irreproachably pure, until the time when we put her in the hands of the man who will see to their happiness. It is for him to lift the veil cast over the sweet secret of life.

But girls [. . .] are often revolted by the somewhat brutal reality hidden behind the dreams. Wounded in their souls, wounded even in their bodies, they refuse their husbands what the law, human law and natural law, accords him as an absolute right. I can't tell you any more about it, my dear; but don't forget this: you belong entirely to your husband.

This sermon, full of allusions and evasions at a time when the very idea of sex education was inconceivable, plunges the bride into a state of dread. Having emerged from the convent, she is about to move directly from the state of innocence to that of a wife. She allows herself to be undressed by her chambermaid and awaits her new husband with the feeling that she has fallen into marriage the way one falls into a bottomless well. The husband knocks softly three times on the door, himself paralysed by an attack of nerves and inexperience. He has come to claim his due, and asks her permission to lie down beside her. She cannot hide her reluctance, he is offended, and goes off to get undressed in the bathroom. He returns in his underwear and slippers and slips into bed. When she feels 'a cold, hairy leg' touching her she stifles a cry. To understand all the piquancy of the situation, one has to realize that at a time when bathing at the seaside was still a privilege reserved for a minority, girls and boys, at least among the well-off classes, had few occasions to examine each other's anatomy; the situation was different in the countryside, where heavy labour performed in common, and seeing animals copulating, caused the young to lose their innocence earlier.

The rest of the night is a disaster. Julien, eager to exercise his right, forces his hand towards Jeanne's breast, and she resists. He becomes impatient, grips her roughly in his arms, and covers her with kisses, finally taking her in what is for her a moment of pain and horror. When he attempts to assault her again, she pushes him away. Thinking with repulsion of the thick hair that covers her husband's chest, she moans: 'So that's what he calls being his wife; it's that, it's that!' Despite an episode of happier sensuality that occurs during a later trip to Corsica, this dreadful night determines the rest of Jeanne's life and ultimately causes her death from 'carnal needs'.

The trauma of the wedding night, which is a mixture of rape and clumsiness, has been replaced by the trial of 'the first time', which is rarely glorious, save for men and women lucky enough to be initiated by charitable souls. It generally takes place between the ages of sixteen and eighteen, the age at which the loss of innocence takes place having remained remarkably stable for the past few decades: boys and girls can now hardly wait to rid themselves of a virginity that handicaps them and slows their entrance into maturity. In the late 1960s, one-third of women were virgins before they married; at the end of the 1980s, only one tenth. Except for Christians, Jews, and fundamentalist Muslims who still assign a symbolic value to the hymen and make its preservation a token of purity, waiting is no longer synonymous with maturation but with stupidity. This is illustrated by Ian McEwan's short novel *On Chesil Beach* (2008), whose action is set in 1962, a few years before the sexual revolution, right in the middle of the transitional period. Edward and Florence, who have just married, have booked lodging in an inn in Dorset, near the beach. Worried about finding themselves alone in their room, they linger over dinner and fear the face-to-face test that awaits them. Florence is revolted by the idea of being naked in the arms of her husband, whom she nonetheless adores, while he knows nothing about sex except masturbation. The night passes and nothing happens; the young couple is paralysed by inhibition. A gesture not made, a word not uttered, and a promising union founders. Chastity is not beautiful, it is grotesque. Because they have not overcome their preconceptions, Edward and Florence destroy their love story: they are not moving, they are pathetic, and the reader laughs at them, glad that he no longer lives in that period.

The revolt against old-fashioned marriage is marked by an inversion of priorities: marriage used to be a matter of self-interest or reason, now it is a matter of inclination, even if considerations of status and money may still be involved. It used to be chaste – 'Marriage is a religious and holy bond', Montaigne said. 'That is why the pleasure we derive from it should be a restrained pleasure, serious, and mixed with some austerity' – now it is sensual for both sexes. It used to be sordidly mercantile – 'Look at the purse, not the face', said a seventeenth-century German proverb from Baden[1] – now it is disinterested. It used to be

1 Quoted by Edward Shorter, *The Making of the Modern Family*. New York: Basic Books, 1975; French trans. Paris: Seuil, 1977, p. 180.

cold – 'Man has two fine days on Earth: when he takes a wife and when he buries her', says another proverb from Anjou that dates from the same period,[2] wife and children counting for less than the livestock, which was a source of profit and food – now it is bathed in mutual affection. It used to be coerced, now it is free. It used to mark a break, the entrance into a new state, today it is often preceded by a trial period of living together. It used to teach renunciation – 'in all things, we must know how to suffer in silence', said a mother to her daughter who was about to marry,[3] to enter into a reclusion in which so many women buried their youth, their hopes –, it claimed to be Edenic, a garden of happiness, a portal leading to mutual fulfilment. It used to require the agreement of the families involved, now it defies their veto even if it is still preferable to have the family's approval.

Everything that was formerly difficult has become simpler, people now become lovers after a few days or weeks, but everything that was once

2 Ibid., French trans., p. 75.
3 Honoré de Balzac, *Mémoires de deux jeunes mariés* (1842). Paris: Folio-Gallimard, p. 170.

taken for granted has become problematic: people deploy Talmudic subtleties in trying to decide whether they are going to move in together, and in what way, whether one partner will accept the keys offered by the other or instead take fright and disappear. The fear of losing one's independence takes priority over the 'modesty' of earlier times. That is the gamble made by modern societies: putting the law in the service of the passions rather than restraining the passions by the law. Founding the durable on the transitory, adopting the slightest inflection of manners and if necessary throwing institutions into turmoil the better to adapt them. Riding the tiger at the risk of being thrown off, channelling by assent the impetuous torrent of emotions that our ancestors held back by prohibitions. A mad ambition whose effects will continue to dog us.

2

Divorce, a 'Judaic Poison'

Since the Enlightenment, marriage reforms have focused on three points: giving priority to feelings over obligation, doing away with the requirement of virginity, and making it easier for badly matched spouses to separate. It was Balzac who, obsessed by female adultery – 'that word [. . .] that drags behind it a dismal cortege, Tears, Shame, Hatred, Terror . . .'[1] and by the vision of millions of husbands 'minotaurized' (that is, cuckolded, given horns) – was to argue for sensual freedom for young people, which alone could provide a remedy for a multitude of evils:

1 Honoré de Balzac, *Physiologie du mariage* (1829). Paris: Folio-Gallimard, p. 19.

Let us restore to the young passions, coqueteries, love and its terrors, love and its sweet pleasures. In that vernal season of life, no mistake is irreparable . . . and love will be justified by useful comparisons. With this change in our manners the shameful plague of prostitution will fade away by itself.

Balzac develops here an argument that was to become classic in the nineteenth century and was also defended by Fourier, Stendhal, and Hugo: obligatory chastity for girls gives rise to the two-fold scourge of sex for money and extramarital affairs, with the terrifying spectre of illegitimacy (in ancient Rome, only pregnant women could engage in infidelities with impunity, because the latter did not put the family line – that is, its spermatic purity – in question). Sex-starved men resorted to brothels, while disappointed wives gave themselves to transitory lovers who were lying in wait for them. In a book that caused a scandal when it appeared in 1907, Léon Blum cleverly plumbed Balzac's proposal: he depicted side by side the virgin

in her sad bed, vainly yearning for the dream of love whose violence or sweetness are exaggerated still further by an ardent imagination, and the prostitute performing on her work-bed, with hurried boredom, a task only too often repeated.[2]

And since each of these two miseries is the condition of the other, the virgin and the prostitute, the latter almost always a working-class woman, they have to be saved together:

One must be made to forget that love exists, while the other must forget that there exists in life anything but love.

The virgin must be denied entrance into sexual life, the prostitute must be forbidden to leave it. And Blum argues, with inspired verve, for the right of girls to sleep around so that they can live out their erotic fantasies with whomever they choose before 'matrimonial maturity' inclines them to marry in a rightful wedding.

Women have bodies, and their bodies need exultation just as men's do. After Balzac, it took more than a century for Western societies, which

2 Léon Blum, *Du mariage*. Paris: Albin Michel, 1990, pp. 248–9.

had in the interim been marked by the Freudian revolution, to acknowledge the reality of feminine Eros, violating the earlier prejudice that preached purity out of fear of lust. Romanticism idealized woman in order to avert the uterine turmoil into which women might sink if they were unfortunately to be given free rein. The dogma of the Immaculate Conception, established by Pius IX in 1854, which declared that Mary was unstained by original sin, can also be understood as a theological lid that was put on the nascent emancipation of women, and that was supposed to incite girls to be continent, like the Virgin.

As for divorce, it was introduced in France by the revolution of 1792, which sought to break the Church's grip on the institution of matrimony. Abolished by the Restoration on 8 May 1816, it was re-established only under the Third Republic in 1884 (but only for just cause) by a law proposed by an 'Israelite' member of the National Assembly, Alfred Naquet. This re-establishment did not fail to elicit furious debates, to the point that the bishop of Angers, in a speech delivered before the Senate on 19 July 1884, uttered the following sentences:

The movement that will lead to the law on divorce is in the true sense of the word a Semitic movement, which began with Monsieur Crémieux and ended with Monsieur Naquet, via a whole group of Israelites, agitators for and promoters of divorce. Well, gentlemen, I still have enough French honour to not lower, so far as I am concerned, Christian civilization's barrier against the Israelites! So go ahead, vote for this law on the side of Israel, go toward the Jews! For our part, we shall remain on the side of the Church and of France.[3]

Less than a century later, the Vichy regime – which saw the Naquet law as the cause of declining birth-rates, the moral and military disaster that had struck France, and other ills – denounced divorce as 'an absolutely Jewish idea', and favoured segregation between Jews and non-Jews.

However, as early as 1664 this Judaic poison was defended by the English poet John Milton, who drew a subtle analogy between the conjugal bond and the national bond: just as a kingdom's

3 Quoted by Rosine Cusset, 'Le mariage saisi par le droit', in *Histoire du mariage*, ed. Sabine Melchior-Bonnet and Catherine Salles. Paris: Robert Laffont, pp. 873–4.

charter can be broken if the sovereign abuses his power or betrays his subjects, marital union can be suspended in the event of serious dissension. At that time, Milton's view caused a strait-laced England to tremble. But after all, Anglicanism itself had been born of a double divorce: Henry VIII's divorce from Catherine of Aragon in order to marry Anne Boleyn, from whom he expected an heir, and the resulting schism with Rome, through which he became the head of the Church of England.

Milton's great idea was later defended by the finest minds of the Enlightenment, such as Diderot, Montesquieu, and Voltaire, with important variations depending on their sensibilities: some authors thought couples should be allowed to divorce only after their children were grown up and emancipated. Helvétius, referring to certain African customs, proposed a trial marriage for three years, whereas Maurice de Saxe proposed one for five years. They all protested the indissolubility advocated by the Catholic Church and railed against a principle that cloistered women, exasperated husbands, and drove both to engage in a sexual promiscuity that threatened to result in multiple illegitimate children. Diderot condemned non-consensual copulation between spouses (which our legal system has renamed 'conjugal rape'):

> I've seen a decent woman shiver with horror at the approach of her husband, I've seen her hasten to bathe and never feel sufficiently cleansed of the stain of her [conjugal] duty. (1772)

3

The Nuptial Utopia

What should we learn from these controversies that lasted at least three centuries and are far from over? That divorce is not an unfortunate accident of marriage but its central axis, since it makes marriage a chosen destiny rather than a prison to be endured. The commitment is all the more authentic because it can be challenged; spouses can go astray with the best will in the world and later correct their error. Their union is based on their decision alone, and it is difficult to maintain if a single party to the contract rejects it (in France, the law of 1 January 2005, seeking to reduce conflict, made it easier to divorce by mutual consent). The possibility of separation spares the couple the dread of being asphyxiated, of the finality of the irrevocable. Just as many desperate people dream of suicide but never actually commit it, the authorization of divorce makes living together less burdensome and makes it possible to put up with monotony: people flirt with escape the better to stay where they are. There are couples who remain together throughout their lives, always threatening to leave but dying hand in hand.

But the benevolence of the eighteenth-century reformers and the revolutionaries of 1792 was not limited to the ambition to provide a remedy for the ills of conjugal life or to prevent men from abandoning their wives encumbered with children. They also had a lyrical vision of feeling, which was supposed to reconcile self-interest, virtue, and happiness, to lead people towards a radiant future. At the end of the Old Regime and up to the middle of the twentieth century, it was reasonable to believe that the passions can be good, provided that they are properly guided: it sufficed to recognize them in order to tame them and make them contribute to social peace. At the beginning of the twentieth century this same hope was reformulated by Léon Blum: he thought that once the last vestige of our bad morals had disappeared and the reforms he demanded had been realized (reforms authorizing women's pre-conjugal sexual experiences in order to prevent any post-nuptial accidents), marriage would endure, accidents would be exceptional, and there would be few divorces.[1] Thus a twofold result would be achieved: the intensity of love and the solidity of the institution of marriage would be allied, and the former would remain under control while breathing its energy into the old matrimonial edifice.

In 1792, in the National Assembly, Citizen Cailly exclaimed:

Divorce will restore marriage's dignity; it will prevent the scandal of separations; it will dry up the source of hatred and cause it to be replaced by love and peace.

The prosecutor Pierre Gaspard Chaumette (a spokesman for the *sans-culottes* who was known

---

1 'I have no difficulty accepting that divorce will continue and even be made easier. In particular, it will be necessary that either of the parties be able to initiate divorce. [. . .] Thus divorces must be easy, but I presume that they will be rare, almost as rare as they are now and perhaps more.' Op. cit., p. 189.

for his enthusiastic endorsement of the guillo-
tine and for his hatred of the Church and the
first feminists, including Olympe de Gouges)
declared that:

> Divorce is the tutelary god of marriage because it
> causes the spouses to enjoy inalterable peace and
> unclouded happiness.[2]

A strange proclamation that makes the dissolution of the bond the very condition of its
continued existence! But the later declaration of
22 August 1795 – the regime had changed in the
meantime – was to establish the family as the
basis of the social contract and proclaim: 'No
one is a good citizen unless he is a good son, a
good father, a good brother, a good friend, and
a good husband.' Seeking to ensure the cohesion
of marriage (divorce was forbidden after twenty
years of living together and when the woman was
past the age of forty-five!), the Napoleonic civil
code considerably restricted the right to divorce

2 Quoted by Ghislaine de Feydeau, 'Un long XIXe siècle. Un
marriage qui résiste et des enjeux qui changent', in *Histoire du
mariage*, op. cit., pp. 641 and 643.

by establishing the minor status of women. The nineteenth century wavered between these two conceptions, incapable of choosing between the fear of feeling and the beauty of the passions, until the twentieth century came down massively on the side of the latter.

The least one can say is that these predictions have proven false. The definition of a new right implies that it is used and abused without limits, but in our part of the world the success of divorce, as soon as it was authorized and simplified, resembled less a readjustment than a tidal wave. In this regard, the statistics are eloquent. In France,[3] the number of marriages has been steadily declining for forty years – 400,000 in 1970; 273,000 in 2008; 265,000 in 2009, whereas the divorce rate is exploding, rising from ten per cent in 1965 to fifty per cent in 2007, a development that remains essentially urban. What would one say about an army that loses half its troops and has difficulty recruiting new soldiers? That it is simply collapsing. Let us add that the majority

3 The same statistics prevail throughout Europe, except on the very Catholic island of Malta, where abortion is still prohibited, though divorce was authorized in 2011 with many restrictions.

of those who initiate divorces are women (almost 70 per cent): since they have achieved financial independence and learned to use contraception, they have less need for men. Their tolerance for the unhappiness and humiliation that used to be visited upon them by despotic husbands has partly vanished, as has the equation of the feminine with resignation.

4

From Forbidden Love to Obligatory Love

Why did a great dream turn into the bankruptcy of the institution it was supposed to protect? We can find one answer to this question in a book by Friedrich Engels published in 1884, *On the Origins of the Family and Private Property*. Engels, Karl Marx's companion in arms, thought that 'the greatest moral progress we owe to monogamy is: modern individual love between the two sexes, which was previously unknown in the world'. After the Revolution, once capitalism and the bourgeoisie have been swept away, he predicts the emergence

of a generation of men who have never been able to purchase the abandonment of a woman by money

or any other means of social power, and of a generation of women who have never been able to give
themselves to a man for any reason other than true
love, or to refuse themselves, out of fear of the economic consequences, to someone they love.

And Engels goes on to defend the right to divorce,
though he adds this fundamental qualification:
'If marriage based on love is the only moral marriage, so is marriage in which love persists.' A
crucial sentence: if feelings fade away the couple
sinks into immorality. They are not advised to get
along, they are ordered to adore one another!

What an irony to see marriage, the emblem of
bourgeois platitude, trying to acquire the flair of
the longing for the absolute, the unconditional!
Love used to be hindered, now it is praised to the
skies, it has become imperative. We have moved
from one dogma to another: marriage arranged
for financial reasons is now prohibited; outside
the reciprocity of emotions, there is no salvation!
Inclination confers on a simple civil contract a
sacredness superior to that provided by a religious
ceremony: marriage becomes a utopia accessible to
all, provided that the heart speaks sincerely. Engels
was not the only writer of his time who issued

such a commandment. A republican member of the French National Assembly, Charles Alric, arguing in 1875 for 'mystical emotion' and effusive communion between spouses, cried:

> It is time for love to become once again what it should never have ceased to be: the determining motive, the essential condition of conjugal union. It alone has the privilege of discerning or creating affinity between persons.[1]

The Christian inspiration of this doctrine is clear, even if the Church has always been wary of the bonfire of the passions. A Catholic author, Edward Montier, a pedagogue and teacher of the young, also wrote in his *Lettre à une jeune fille* (1919), a long plea for sentimentalism in the working class: 'Love, that is the divine gift, the infinite treasure that re-establishes the balance between all men.' It will be recalled, perhaps, that the worldly hero of this upheaval was to be King Edward VIII, who preferred to abdicate on 11 December 1936 to marry an American woman,

1 Quoted by Jean-Claude Bologne in *Histoire du mariage en Occident.* Paris: Hachette Pluriel, 1995, p. 356.

Wallis Simpson – a divorcee who, it was said, had been for a time the mistress of Joachim von Ribbentrop, Hitler's future minister (the king himself was an overt Nazi sympathizer) – rather than pursue a secret affair on the side. Swoons are well worth a throne!

The disorder of our morals is generally attributed to the triumph of the consumerist spirit, which propagates ephemeral adventures. What if it were the other way round? What if it were the liberation of love that explains our disarray, since we superimpose the rehabilitation of the heart peculiar to Romanticism on the 1960s rehabilitation of the body? To put it another way: up to the Second World War, marriage killed love. Since then, love has been fatal not only to marriage, which has been in free fall for the past thirty years, but also to the very possibility of the couple, of which marriage is only a magnifying mirror. All the criticisms addressed to the former now apply to the latter: the possibility of two people living a life in common has been put in question again.[2]

2 In the United States, where remarriage is very frequent, the divorce rate is 47.9 per cent, according to statistics provided

Conjugal life used to be a prison in which women wasted away; at the beginning of his novel *Thérèse Desqueyroux* (1927), François Mauriac speaks eloquently of the 'living prison bars' of a family. The walls have been torn down, and now we carry the prison in ourselves: it is called 'perfect love'. How beautiful the latter used to be, in chains, adorned with all the virtues. It had only to be liberated to carry in its wake as many disasters as joys. Why does it seem so difficult to endure these days? Because we venerate it like a deity, because it has become, like happiness, the alpha and omega of our Western societies. Set up an idol and you immediately engender millions of misfits who are incapable of rising to such heights and who think they are deficient. Even flesh has to maintain its rank, prove itself, we want our thrills to be erudite, militant. Fornication, a crime in the Middle Ages. is now a source of pride, a test of self-fulfilment. Just as people make themselves unhappy because they

by the United States Health Department. It is highest in the very religious states of the 'Bible Belt', where social and religious conventions incite people to marry very early, without knowing what they are doing. Divorce is also exploding in Asian countries that are experiencing an economic boom.

are not happy, they worry about never knowing 'mad love' (André Breton's *amour fou*), a terrible expression that celebrates not the heart but the trance: any affection that isn't mad isn't worthy of being experienced.

Thus we have sought to conflate love and marriage, to tame the latter, to make the former more supple: we marry less, we divorce more, and we prefer free relationships or cohabitation so that we can shape our feelings as we wish. There is no longer any need to get married in order to live together or have children. In most European countries, the wedding ceremony has become simply useless. From this we can draw a twofold lesson: we have made access to the married state so easy that we have ceased to consider it desirable. But no matter how discreet the straitjacket, it is still too tight and increases our resistance to the remaining constraints. We will not return to the forced marriages of earlier times, of which many religions and societies provide horrifying examples. But nothing prohibits us from envisaging the return of unions based on self-interest, provided they are freely chosen by the two partners. The choice is not between reason and passion, but between consent and constraint.

It has to be acknowledged, then, that our conquests come at a price, and we have to conceive our progress in the form of partial regressions, not univocal advances. What was supposed to produce felicity also produces distress. The doubt we feel does not arise from a defeat but from a victory: love has indeed triumphed over marriage, but now it is destroying it from inside. The new world looks very much like the old one, the heart is prey to the same torment and indecision. Past centuries oscillated between praise for sensibility and the condemnation of the passions: we have entered the age of perplexity. The conflict has not been eradicated, as had been hoped; it is being continued at another level. Many literary works and films testify to this: even if it is more straightforward, the contemporary landscape of love is not as euphoric or light-hearted. As in the past, infidelity, loss, and betrayals are central to the plots, and the disenchantment is all the greater because marriages are voluntary and not imposed. Married life used to be a prison cell; now it seems be transforming itself into a sobering-up cell. We have not found the remedy for the sufferings of love, any more than our ancestors did.

5

The Pathologies of the Ideal

The tragedy of the marriage of inclination is that it seeks to normalize the exceptional, to make it the rule, to transform attachment, in accord with the old evangelical credo, into the value of all values, a gold standard of morality. Then it is preferable to castigate the market and individualism rather than touch this idol and indict it. The whole problem arises from the fact that we cannot say anything about love without saying the opposite at the same time. That is what is fearsome and fascinating about love: it is a portmanteau word, it designates abnegation as much as egoism, desire as much as sublimation, whims as much as constancy. It is at once the gamble of establishing eternity within time, the set of forces that resists erosion and forgetting, and the instantaneous flaring-up of the senses and of souls. It is the desire for incandescence as much as the desire for permanence, and both are equally valid. Only a lazy philosophy could celebrate love's unqualified goodness, its good will par excellence, and see in it the solution to all our problems. Its marvellous complexity in French has to be preserved; otherwise it will be taken over by force, imprisoned in a maximalist definition and sanitized, made inaccessible to ordinary mortals.

In this respect, to judge a couple solely by the yardstick of vehemence is to condemn it to insufficiency; it is to tell lovers: you don't love the way you're supposed to, because you have to have emotions that grip you, you don't know anything, you have to relearn everything. It is to favour professors of rectification who are assigned to put our free-wheeling affections back on track. In order to repair our imperfect relationships, they advise us to breathe still more passion into our lives: to cure the disease, they recommend injecting the patient with an additional dose of poison. You might as well try to put out a fire with petrol! Trading in discord, these specialists, coaches, therapists, and 'crisis managers' often sell us at a high price the recipes that used to be offered by popular wisdom: make concessions, talk to one another, be attentive to your partner, surprise him with little gestures. The homily competes with the commonplace. The intense, faithful love they advocate would ruin them if it were ever realized, just as dentists and doctors would disappear if diseases and caries were eradicated.

Consider this current dream: everything in one, everything or nothing. A single person has to condense the totality of our aspirations, and if he fails to do so, we get rid of him. The madness lies in wanting to reconcile everything, the heart and eroticism, raising children and social success, effervescence and the long term. Our couples are not dying of selfishness and materialism, they're dying of a fatal heroism, an excessively great conception of themselves. This grandiose vision tears them apart the way prisoners are torn by barbed wire. Every woman has to be simultaneously a mother, a whore, a friend, and a fighter, every man has to be a father, a lover, a husband, and a provider: watch out for those who don't fulfil these conditions! To the reasons generally given to explain conjugal unhappiness, we must add another very contemporary toxin: immoderate ambition. Couples go aground like an overloaded ship: they try to conform, to remain on the summits of ardour, while at the same time taking care of everyday business. Have pity on them! The mythologies of paroxysm reflect on the level of psychological drives the same mechanisms of yield that are at work in the economic or financial domains.

So flee like the plague those who cry: 'I'm an idealist!' because that assertion means in reality: I have lofty pretensions, I am not content with people of little value. I will judge you by the laws of a pitiless tribunal. Under the apparent nobility of such remarks we have to hear the verdict of a fanatical prosecutor who is dying to reject you. It isn't you that he's evaluating, it's your greater or lesser conformity to his ideal. A mad Platonism: we are to love love more than the persons themselves, seek it through interchangeable individuals instead of cherishing one individual unlike any other. Slander our current relationships in the name of an imaginary fusion, as if there were no one for whom it is worth giving up our freedom. My hopes are never adequately met, never adequately rewarded, I deserve better.

Everyone knows the horrible proverb: the most beautiful woman in the world can give only what she has. But what she has is already so marvellous that one ought to bow down before her to thank her for granting it to us.

A terrible absurdity: living as a couple has become more difficult to endure since of all its roles it has retained only that of being a model of fulfilment. Because it wants to succeed at any cost, it is consumed with anxiety, fears the law of entropy, the aridity of slack periods. The slightest decrease in tension is experienced as a fiasco, a rejection. Adoration is put to the test of its own defeat insofar as it is realized, that is, normalized. Valuing frenzy, we put the married couple in danger: the bond literally melts under the empire of fever, the borderlines between the other and the self tend to become blurred. The domestic sphere has become the stake in a titanic battle between the sublimity sought and the trivial felt. Crazy love, says the orthodox view spread by the media, magazines, and advertising; hazy love lovers ought to reply. That is, love that doesn't know where it is, that doesn't want to decide between its definitions, that doesn't care whether it will be great or small, routine or risky, passing or persevering. Passionate love is the love of passion, that is, of torment; it is war, constant demand, the reign of the highest bidder, a face-to-face encounter forever. Hardly has the word been uttered than images of squalls, tears, cries, and resounding ecstasies rise up; but if it is to endure, we also need gaiety, regularity, and enthusiasm. In order to live together, there is no need to adore each other in the canonical sense of the term; it suffices to like each other, to share the same tastes, to seek all the happiness possible in the framework of a harmonious coexistence. If we want it to last, let's stop subjecting life in common to the despotic law of exuberance.

There are several, equally legitimate ways of being fond of one another, however much we may otherwise be tempted to judge negatively those that differ from our own. This judgement is not always moral; it may also arise from anxiety: what if I made a mistake, what if I made the wrong choice? All couples are enigmas for one another, in their failures as in their resurrections. Some are too demonstrative and wither away from an excess of symbiosis; some that are less well suited may go on, off kilter, for years; some may be kept going by an unbridled social ambition, some poisonous ones spread destruction and devastation, some friendly ones offer themselves to all their admirers; some grow together and envelop themselves in the joy of their reciprocal inflation; and some, whose generosity flows over their entourage, galvanize.

6

Honey and Hemlock

The increase in the rate of divorce underscores the paradoxical success of marriage for love, from which so much is expected – plenitude and sensual pleasure – that we are ready to break it off at the first hitch. Whereas arranged marriage elicits few illusions, and thus is less likely to disappoint. It is mostly wives, as we have seen, who leave, even in times of crisis, even if the break entails a sudden decrease in income and a risk of being left alone after the age of fifty. It still seems stupefying that people who enjoy the privileges of a comfortable life would choose, against their most elementary interests, to give up everything and start all over.[1] That is the tragedy of certain separations: you want to try again, tremble on the brink of the abyss, and put your frail happiness in the hands of a stranger who breaks your heart. It's the crazy pleasure of devastation, but it's preferable to those sad couples who, because they don't have the means to rent separate residences, continue to live under the same roof even though they are allergic to each other. There are also men and women who don't break up but instead accumulate, setting up their ex-partners in their homes or next door because they are incapable of cutting the tie, and who live in phalansteries, watching over the collection of people they have loved.

In this group hungry for novelty we may distinguish the tribe of supercharged retirees (two categories of couples break up in France, the very young and those over fifty).[2] Rather well-off, if they belong to the middle or upper classes, and in

1 According to the statistics, the loss of income during a separation is supposed to be between 15 and 20 per cent for each of the partners. Some CEOs declare bankruptcy to avoid paying a compensatory indemnity.

2 See Jacqueline Rémy's very illuminating article 'Mon amour, c'est la crise. Et si l'on divorçait?' in *Marianne*, 26 November–4 December 2009). Her investigation shows that contrary to Anglo-Saxons, who defer breakups in a recession, the French, when the value of their holdings is falling, separate on all sides, paying no attention to economic uncertainty.

good health, they are eager to sink their teeth into life, and they go through a frantic post-adolescence at an age when their ancestors were already senile or bedridden. Both sexes may be struck at any time by follies of the heart and mind: Viagra has broken up more than one marriage by offering resigned senior citizens intoxicating powers that stir up peaceful lower parts and resuscitate an organ that seemed to have become fossilized. The same possibilities will soon be offered to women. The gluttony of the elderly who roll the dice one last time, shed their life companions, and throw themselves into sports, travel, and carnal saturnalia, also proceeds from increased longevity. A marvellous conquest: whereas in Europe, the average age at which women first give birth has reached thirty, and the 'endpoint marked by menopause' may someday be abolished, each of us is offered a whole strategic temporal depth: an opportunity to lead several successive lives, to put off until later what used to be done in youth.

The Great New Beginning is the only form of eternity we have found in our world since the belief in Paradise faded away, even among the faithful. Each of us has several lives in the course of his or her existence, and these lives do not resemble one another. We have the right to make mistakes and correct them, we have the right to 'fail, fail again, fail better' (Samuel Beckett). What is finer than short-circuiting traditional temporal sequences in order to snub your nose at destiny, granting yourself, at least for a few years, an extra portion of heady pleasures, sensations, and encounters? The game goes on right up to your last day, and that's why the second or third marriage is generally more successful than the first. What a difference from the nineteenth century, when one of Balzac's heroines could exclaim: 'I'm thirty years old, and the warmest part of the day is already behind me, the hardest part of the road already travelled. In a few years, I'll be an old woman . . .'[3]

Today, you're young until you get old: the age of adulthood has disappeared in this operation. It is the idea of maturity itself that has been eclipsed, we sow our wild oats contrary to the biological clock, young people shack up together at twenty, whereas their parents flirt and have one affair after another. Léon Blum, it will be

3 Honoré de Balzac, *Mémoires de deux jeunes mariés*, op. cit., p. 265.

resemble one another. We have the right to make mistakes and correct them, we have the right to 'fail, fail again, fail better' (Samuel Beckett). What is finer than short-circuiting traditional temporal sequences in order to snub your nose at destiny, granting yourself, at least for a few years, an extra portion of heady pleasures, sensations, and encounters? The game goes on right up to your last day, and that's why the second or third marriage is generally more successful than the first. What a difference from the nineteenth century, when one of Balzac's heroines could exclaim: 'I'm thirty years old, and the warmest part of the day is already behind me, the hardest part of the road already travelled. In a few years, I'll be an old woman . . .'[3]

Today, you're young until you get old: the age of adulthood has disappeared in this operation. It is the idea of maturity itself that has been eclipsed, we sow our wild oats contrary to the biological clock, young people shack up together at twenty, whereas their parents flirt and have one affair after another. Léon Blum, it will be

3 Honoré de Balzac, *Mémoires de deux jeunes mariés*, op. cit., p. 265.

6

Honey and Hemlock

The increase in the rate of divorce underscores the paradoxical success of marriage for love, from which so much is expected – plenitude and sensual pleasure – that we are ready to break it off at the first hitch. Whereas arranged marriage elicits few illusions, and thus is less likely to disappoint. It is mostly wives, as we have seen, who leave, even in times of crisis, even if the break entails a sudden decrease in income and a risk of being left alone after the age of fifty. It still seems stupefying that people who enjoy the privileges of a comfortable life would choose, against their most elementary interests, to give up everything and start all over.[1] That is the tragedy of certain separations: you want to try again, tremble on the

recalled, counted on a calming of the passions after a certain age that would make couples better suited to a permanent relationship. But we don't get wiser as we get older, and mid-life crises can strike at any time up to the day of death. That's what has changed: we're hungrier for pleasures than ever before, and everything seems possible at any time.

7

The Round of Disappointed Lovers

It is less the bitterness of love that we should fear than its versatility, its reversals that make you trample on what you adored and that kindle passions for others. Just as we idolize, we forget; just as we neglect, we are excited. Eros is the power of life, the god that brings together, and among the ancients it is Eris (discord) and Kairos (opportunity) as well as Cupid, the blind archer who shoots his arrows at random and wreaks havoc everywhere. Foreseeing all this, the Princess of Clèves does not yield, even after the death of her husband, to Monsieur de Nemours, a notorious seducer who would soon be unfaithful to her if she made him her lover. His fervour, having declined after the initial infatuation, would soon be directed towards a new object:

Up to that time she had not known the stings of mistrust and jealousy; her only thought had been to keep from loving Monsieur de Nemours, and she had not yet begun to fear that he loved another. [. . .] She was astounded that she had never yet thought how improbable it was that a man like Monsieur de Nemours, who had always treated women with such fickleness, should be capable of a sincere and lasting attachment. [. . .] Do I wish to expose myself to the cruel repentance and mortal anguish that are inseparable from love?[1]

The Princess of Clèves is not a paragon of virtue, a crusader for fidelity, but rather a model of prudence who prefers the icy solitude of widowhood to the risks of a tumultuous love life. In 1784, Kant referred to the 'unsociable sociability' of men that leads them to enter into society even though they find the company of others repugnant. Chemists, Goethe remarked, used to be called 'separators' or analysts. They took the elements apart in order to form new ones, and their science, which was then in full flight, served Goethe as a model in

1 Marie-Madelaine de Lafayette, *The Princess of Clèves*, trans. T. S. Perry and J. D. Lyons. New York: Norton, 1994, p. 64

his novel *Elective Affinities* (1809), in which he described human relations as subject to the forces of magnetic attraction and repulsion. But could he foresee the extraordinary tempest to which the liberation of the passions was about to give rise in Europe?

Besides, it's better to laugh about it; our failures are as comical as they are painful. In our great metropolises, our manners resemble a permanent vaudeville show: dramatic reversals, poignant aches, sombre ruminations, catfights, hasty couplings followed by new heartbreaks. In certain classes in urban centres, the children of undivorced parents can be counted on the fingers of one hand, while other children, carrying a perpetually packed bag, move back and forth between father and mother in accord with the agreements made. Depending on our mood, we can see in this a landscape in ruins or testimony to a great refinement. The rapid combustion of our libidos and our hearts explains the infernal round of couples that are formed and undone, not to mention the mimetic separations that lead whole groups to split up by imitation.

With this epidemic of break-ups and hook-ups, we enter into the comedy of repetition reproduced in the millions of copies, as if an invisible choreographer were commanding everyone to move from wonder to disappointment and back again. We seek each other and at the same time try to flee, we alternate infatuation and cooling off, and celibacy is proliferating in large cities in proportion to population density and the temptations on offer. Thus in our part of the world, especially among young urban adults, more and more people of all ages and conditions are waiting for someone to turn up – in France, an immense reserve army of hearts, some fourteen million 'singles'. That may be the fatal equation of our time: a crossing of futility with intransigence. Our taste for the absolute also makes us fickle, because we expect everything from love, which has become the secular form of Salvation.

8

Towards Separation in a State of Euphoria?

Divorce has its fanatics, its martyrs, and its apos-
tles. Some people celebrate it as a bash to which
you should invite your friends, and in Great
Britain lists of divorces can even be published
in certain magazines in order to help each partner start over. In Paris, a salon for married and
unmarried couples (*Pacs*) held in November
2009 was followed for the first time by a salon for
divorce, separation, and widowhood, under the
title *New Departure*. This determined effort to
put a positive spin on an extremely painful event
reminds us of the episode in *Alice in Wonderland*
in which the queen bleeds before she has been
cut and is healed before she has suffered. Thus
you might be able to separate even before making

44

a commitment, and on your wedding day law-
yers would have you sign, in the name of the
precautionary principle, liquidation documents.
Isn't it going too far to make divorce, even if one
approves of it, an occasion for jubilation, as if the
break-up were more beautiful than the wedding?
Or to collect divorces as a source of pride, the
way Soviet marshals used to parade about with
their chests covered in medals? The conversion
of trouble into exhilaration is typical of a whole
school of obligatory optimism that refuses to see
anything but opportunities to be seized where
common sense detects distress. You've just lost
your job? Lucky devil, a multitude of opportunities is open to you! You've been diagnosed with
cancer? Be happy about it, this disease is going
to change you radically. Your wife has left you?
Hallelujah, you're free!

Don't take things so seriously, that's the motto.
'If he leaves me, that very night I'll log onto
Meetic.' This comment made by a young woman
regarding her inconstant lover is symptomatic
of a certain view of the slimmed-down individual whom nothing affects, who recovers from
everything, even the worst, a perpetual spring of
freedom without memory or pain, a pure creative

impulse. In a society of self-invention, there is no longer any tragedy, only contracts made and broken, that's what this new ideology tells us. Too bad about the great victims of break-ups, the spouses abandoned, the children who are transported from one family to another to re-acclimate them like plants in a pot. In economics, the Austrian philosopher Friedrich Hayek used the term 'catalexy' to refer to the market's conversion of the enemy into a friend; what name should we give to the inverse movement which, in the conjugal couple, transforms two turtle-doves into irreconcilable enemies? Deifying the other means that he will soon be knocked off his pedestal, cast to the ground, turned into a devil. 'Of all sentiments, love is the most selfish and consequently, when it is wounded, the least generous' (Benjamin Constant). It's a terrible thing, that accumulation of hatred that floats around some old married couples like a lethal gas ready to explode (as in Granier-Deffere's film *Le Chat*)! Why split up? To regain peace and control over one's own life, but also to feel once again the vibration of being in love, to rediscover the emotion of the first time. Then we are prepared to do anything to get rid of the person who hems us in and embodies everything we have given up. As if he had to pay a high price for no longer inspiring us, and as if the nastiness of announcing the break-up had to be accompanied by the boorishness of the way of doing it (the worst being, perhaps, leaving one morning without saying a word after twenty or thirty years of living together, walking out the door and never coming back).

Why should we be surprised that some separations drive people mad and lead to extreme reactions, and that some divorced people resemble boxers stunned by roundhouse punches? For example, the Frenchman who, having been ordered by the court to share all his possessions with his ex-wife, sawed in two all the furniture, televisions, computers, and carpets in their apartment (repeating, perhaps without knowing it, a scene in Robert Altman's film *Short Cuts*). In Germany, some telephone companies offer to handle the separation for you, in order to spare you painful scenes and annoyance. All desertions are difficult, but some are inelegant and even abject: for instance, leaving a partner who is seriously ill, or leaving your first wife who has shared all your hardships, hung on for years, and sacrificed her own studies and hopes, so that you can go off with a younger woman, or repudiating your husband the moment he receives his pink slip, or leaving him for his best friend. We find it legitimate to leave a partner but atrocious to be 'cut loose' (the word reflects the terror of being left adrift). For people who have been dumped and whose only crime is having lived with you, the love that unites and the freedom that liberates become the love that separates and the freedom that oppresses. He or she leaves me, and on top of that, has the backing of the law. The law is nothing without morals, but morals ask the laws to confirm what they are, how far they can go. The famous phrase recited in the wedding ceremony, 'For better or for worse', could be reformulated this way: 'for the better; otherwise, too bad'.

Nations as well have acquired the right to divorce one another: their ties correspond to the same principle of floating union as those between individuals, and their separations are no less dramatic. There are countries in which cohabitation under the same roof is merely a prelude to separation (Belgium), others that cling fiercely to their single status (Switzerland and the European Union), some that retain separate rooms but sleep in the same bed (Germany), and some that limit themselves to prudent engagements while postponing marriage indefinitely (Turkey and Europe). And finally, there are countries that threaten to pack their bags and are always about to leave (Quebec within Canada). There is an underestimated conjugal dimension of political life at the moment when the bond between the citizen and the state is contractualised as well. Nations have become as fragile as the citizens who compose them; they have lost the coherence they thought they had. The more the Earth shrinks, the more human tribes aspire to distance themselves from one another: they are suffocating on a globe that is as chock-full as the closed sphere of marriage.

9

A Ministry of Broken Hearts?

Prostitution, adultery; for the past two centuries, how many reformers have promised that these plagues would be eradicated once we got beyond bourgeois marriage! But they have persisted, as have lying, dissimulation, jealousy, and possessiveness. We can be scandalized, or we can try to understand. Venality is explained by poverty, low salaries, and the appetite for easy money among those who practise prostitution as a profession or a source of supplemental income; so far as customers, male or female (because these days women also pay for sexual services) are concerned, we can give two reasons for this persistence: the pleasure taken in an immediate eroticism without consequences, and the comforting feeling of being accepted despite one's physical defects (think of the actor Michel Simon's enlightening remark thanking prostitutes for having accepted him in spite of his ugly face). Both sexes will continue to pay for sex, no matter how sordid it is, so long as men and women want to engage in an interlude of sensual pleasure or spare themselves, by paying for their sexual needs, the wounds inflicted by a rejection.

As for adultery, which used to be the symbol of revolt against forced marriages, it reflects a taste for distraction, shortcuts for those who are bored by marriage and are unable to resist temptations. To judge by the omnipresence of this theme in film and literature, and the suffering it provokes, the candidates must be legion. Sometimes, out of a taste for secrecy, people deceive those whom they love in order to reassure, distract, or rejuvenate themselves, and this infidelity, equally shared by both halves of humanity, is called curiosity, vanity, narcissism, and a boundless appetite for new bodies. Feminism also defends women's right to embrace men's mistakes and to add to them. The fact that oppression was horrible does not mean that liberation is going to prove to be marvellous.

So should we turn the screw a little further and return to the old regimes of desire? Should we, for instance, establish a Ministry of Broken Hearts that would punish the fickle and console those who have been abandoned? (Among certain feminists, a desire to chastise womanizers the better to absolve faithless wives can be discerned.) Should we, as some jurists demand, establish a right not to be abandoned or a right to be abandoned with dignity, or else defer divorce until the couple's children have reached adulthood? In California, certain groups of citizens are trying to abolish divorce altogether, and since 1997 the state of Louisiana, followed by Arkansas and Arizona, has sought to further restrict divorce by means of the Covenant Marriage Law, a statute that has biblical accents but no noticeable effects on reality. It is not possible to pass laws on the appalling aspects of feeling without legislating regarding its good aspects as well. We can increase economic protection for abandoned spouses and concern ourselves with their children's welfare, but we can't prevent separations! In 2009 a French government minister suggested penalizing 'grey marriages', that is, 'sentimental swindles with the goal of obtaining residency papers' in which one person pretends to adore another in order to obtain economic advantages, identity papers, gifts of money, or real estate, but this overlooks the fact that every sentimental relationship implies a risk of being deceived. To fall in love with someone is to give him permission to mislead us with our consent. The concentration of our desires on a precise individual implies that we invent him as much as we discover him, at the risk of embellishing him in the process of this re-creation. The greatest scams always use the idiom of fervour, of devotion. Even if the other person is sincere at the moment when he tells you that he loves you, nothing guarantees that he will keep his promise, because he is no more in control of his emotions than you are. In this area we cannot ask each partner to provide in advance proof of his present and future attachment. Criminalizing the sphere of intimacy means allowing the state to interfere in a private agreement, and, by supervising our deepest hearts, to take over our role as guarantors of promises or good conduct. All those arrivistes, both male and female, who generally come from underprivileged classes or poor countries and use their charms to seduce people with influence and climb the social ladder, offering their youth and erotic expertise in exchange for financial security – what law could prohibit them? How can we not understand them? We always love in a precise social and political context in which differences of status and income, if they are too great, interfere more or less with the impulses of the heart and the communion of souls.

Let us avoid drawing hasty conclusions: monogamy, it is said, is not humanity's natural impulse. But neither is polygamy. And that's the whole problem: so long as monogamy continues to structure life as a couple, the risk of deception has a bright future. But if polygamy were to become obligatory, many people would take refuge in a strict and almost neurotic loyalty. The real adulterous threesome today is the husband, the wife, and the lawyer who can turn against either of the other two, indifferently, depending on who pays his fees. There is no human nature, there is only a principle of uncertainty, a desire that does not always know what it wants. Long before Freud, this ambivalence was the great lesson of clear-sightedness taught by the French moralists. The beauty of their maxims seems sometimes to contradict the pessimism of their assertions. Even though they say that human nature is bad, that 'the heart of man is hollow and full of filth' (Pascal), they limit themselves to confirming the dogma of original sin, and remain reliant on the dominant religion of their times. The elegance of their formulas is enough to acquit humans and foretells a possible redemption in God. Despite their genius, their work is not in the tragic mode: the latter begins with the hope of a better world to be realized by humans who are solely responsible for their failures. The great love novels themselves are always written against love; just think of Flaubert, Proust, Zweig, Tanizaki, Duras, Albert Cohen, or Kundera, all of whom explore its dark, tragic side. These brilliant clinicians tell us more about the reality of love than any number of bland treatises; while tearing it to shreds they do it indirect homage, recognizing its power to spellbind as well as to destroy. That is the splendour of literature: it looks human misery in the face and draws from it an opportunity for enjoyment and understanding.

We have 'liberated' love, and now we have to teach it, in all its richness and refinements, to a younger generation corrupted by the two-fold discourse of cheap romanticism and X-rated films. Sex education in grammar schools is a good thing, but it would be even better to read and reread poets, novelists, and moralists to make the attraction of hearts something more than an accumulation of quiverings or a slapdash contact of epidermises (according to the Obin report published in 2004, Rousseau and *Madame Bovary* cannot be studied in certain French secondary schools because they are immoral). The emotional poverty of many urban areas inhabited by the working classes and immigrants, which are being eaten away by a combination of religious obscurantism and pornographic discourse, should be combated in the schools, which are destroyers of prejudices and providers of nuances. At a time when 'the culture of the rabble' seems to be invading all levels of society, including that of the children of the middle classes, and leading to an impoverishment of the vocabulary and to violent conduct, it would be a genuine contribution to public health to give the emotions a language capable of expressing all sorts of subtleties.

10

An Agony Amidst Glory

We should not exaggerate the moral dissolution deplored by a crotchety conservatism. Lamentations on the solitude of our contemporaries, a cliché of a certain kind of sociology, forget that it has become, especially for women, a right that supersedes the old pact of servitude. The anathema that not so long ago was fulminated against single people, divorcees, and young widows, accusing them of leading sinful lives and harbouring wicked designs, is no longer. These days, we are more alone because we are more free, even if this freedom is accompanied by anxiety; it is not clear that we would tolerate the constraints and petty annoyances that obtained in earlier times.

But above all, marriages last, at least half of them, and couples stay together, if not because they are overflowing with affection, at least because they find it advantageous to do so. We can assume that had divorce been authorized in its present forms in the nineteenth century, wives eager to free themselves from the suffocating bonds of marriage would have resorted to it in large numbers. The pious stability that we admire in past centuries was a stability of coercion that we would no longer want. Finally, the crisis of the institution of marriage goes hand in hand, as we have seen, with its great attraction: outside Europe, for the middle and upper classes that aspire to escape traditions and families (whence the large number of interracial or inter-faith marriages in countries with strong ethnic or denominational tensions), and within Europe, for gays and lesbians, who have made it, along with adoption, the last stage in gaining recognition. A clever strategy: the margin does not seek to destroy the norm, but to broaden it to behaviours that the norm heretofore described as deviant or against nature. This is the whole paradox: marriage is dying, as it were, in full health, in a glorious triumph. Perhaps it no longer has the majesty of a sacrament, but it will always be more than an administrative formality; it is not subject to contractual neutrality. More than ever, it embodies a problem and an anchorage: the more freedom is extended, the more the need for structures that can channel the erotic impulses of our desires grows. Even the alternatives to marriage do it homage; like a dying star, marriage sheds its light on the satellites around it.

Consider the unexpected success of the 'pact of civil solidarity' (*Pacs*) instituted in France in 1999. Originally intended only for homosexuals, to provide for the transmission of property from one partner to another, for most heterosexuals it has now become almost the equivalent of a marriage engagement. Even if the pact has a high rate of dissolution and one partner can withdraw from it unilaterally by sending a certified letter, with it we remain on the verge of engagement: let's bond, but not too much, so that we can enjoy the dizzy pleasure of the first moments. Let the grace of improvisation take precedence over the weight of established fact. Let's remain in the poetry of lovers to avoid sinking into the prose of spouses! In this way, all sorts of substitutes for marriage multiply, adopting its symbolism without its gravity and offering the advantages of the institution, but in the garb of insubordination (only tax laws still remain disadvantageous for unmarried couples). Which shows that statism goes hand in hand with individualism; we need that anonymous power that helps us grow up, aids us without our having to thank it.

Squaring the circle: the contemporary citizen wants to be protected by the state and protected from the state. Leave me alone when everything is going well, but take care of me when I get in trouble. This forces the legislator eager to follow the development of morals to invent all sorts of legal excrescences and neologisms whose multitude merely reflects the chaos of our aspirations. The crisis of marriage concerns us all, as we have said, because it is first of all the crisis of the couple, and the remedies proposed for its ills are generally limited to reproducing it on the sly. Our lexical quandary, when we try to introduce to others the person with whom we are living without being married, is revealing: companion, friend, fiancé, lover – all these terms that belong to the register of euphemism or modesty show how hard it is for us to think outside the conjugal bond at the very moment that we seem to be rejecting it. A fine symptom of this was seen when Simone de Beauvoir, an advocate of free love, affectionately called her American lover, Nelson Algren, 'my husband'.[1]

1 Simone de Beauvoir, *Lettres à Nelson Algren*. Paris: Gallimard, 1997, p. 169.

II

The Liberating Tradition

On 22 August 2009, a large meeting organized by the Islamic High Council took place in a stadium in Bamako, Mali, to protest against a reform of family law passed by the parliament that proposed to raise the age of marriage for girls from thirteen to eighteen, in order to prevent abuses and to re-establish a certain form of equity between the two sexes. The protestors, who numbered 50,000, held up signs bearing this slogan: 'Western civilization is a sin.' We can laugh at this demonization, the eternal alibi of fundamentalists of every stripe: hatred of the West is always ultimately a hatred of freedom, because only the West has dared challenge its own traditions, to free itself from abuses disguised as customs, and to wage war on its own barbarity, inviting the rest of the world to follow suit.

But is the destruction of the patriarchal order as we have practised it directly applicable to every culture (assuming that European-style emancipation is the only path for the rest of the world to follow)? Isn't it necessary to arrange transitions adapted to the historical context? A development that took centuries in the West is supposed to be compressed into a few in societies that are called upon to reject age-old prejudices and habits. That is the whole problem of Islam in Europe and North America, which has had to accept in the course of a few decades the secularism, religious choice, and liberation of morals that it took the West four centuries of bitter struggles to achieve. Overturning by simple decree the old hierarchical edifice regulating the relationships between the sexes is sometimes, in countries not prepared for it, an upheaval that leads to panic.

Thus we must support the rights of women and minorities wherever they are flouted, and at the same time take into account, flexibly, the non-concordance of times and mentalities. The disappropriation of women's bodies regarding questions of filiation, sexuality, and abortion is a symbolic stake that arouses, in traditional societies, the most violent and hideous resistance (including the continuation of practices of genital mutilation and lapidation, the wearing of the burqa, the rejection of coeducation, and polygamy).[1] If there is nothing we can do about these barbarous customs outside our borders except denounce them, we can do everything possible to make them illegal in Europe and crack down with the greatest severity on those who continue to practise them. No compromise in the name of culturalist arguments is possible in this case. In Europe, the twentieth century witnessed a revolt against the father and patriarchy. The twenty-first century will be a period of revolt against the mother and matriarchy, because science is currently dispossessing women of their control over fecundity and we may soon be able to produce children in the laboratory. Thereafter

1 In France, some imams organize, in a spirit of competition with the registry office, lightning marriages of a few days or weeks for the faithful who are engaging in brief affairs while traveling, a sort of 'sexual channel surfing certified halal', as one of them put it. There are two kinds of polygamy in France: a residual one proceeding from sub-Saharan Africa, and another, militant one proceeding from fundamentalist Muslims who want to assert the superiority of religious faith over the republican legal code.

relationships between the two halves of humanity will be re-established on new foundations.

Unless Western civilization is overthrown by a fundamentalist Islam entrenched in its European bastions and carrying with it in its wake, by a kind of domino effect, all Christian, Jewish, and Buddhist moral authorities – an outcome that currently seems unlikely – there is no solution to be found in returning to the past. But there was a wisdom in ancient customs that we would do well to take as our inspiration while not suffering from the oppression that accompanied them. Modernity's gigantic project of 'creative destruction' sometimes requires pauses or compromises. Let's count on an intelligent conservatism that seeks to reconcile concern for freedom with a flexible fidelity to certain traditions. Not everything in the latter was oppressive, and not everything in innovation is liberating. Some habits forged in the course of centuries deserve to be continued; they combine in themselves a civilizing process, the genius and the memory of many generations. We can add to the egalitarianism of the present a few customs of the past, especially since the harshness of earlier conjugal life has often been exaggerated; it was not always deprived of sweetness and amenity. Just as we have to avoid celebrating the good old days in order to condemn the current period, we have to be wary of describing the past as purely obscurantist, as if we had the right to judge it from the vantage point of our superior understanding. Are we to suppose that our ancestors wandered in the dark for millennia before we finally arrived at the truth? What arrogance! Chroniclers, letters, and great novels testify to the fact that earlier unions, at least in certain milieus, did not lack either a tenderness or a happiness to which only death put an end. The American historian Edward Shorter mentions peasant couples in Old Regime France in which the wife, as her husband's servant, stood behind him as he ate, waiting silently until he had finished before sitting down to eat in her turn.[2] In a striking commentary, Shorter wonders whether the spouses, who had to do heavy labour and were exhausted and used up before their time, didn't sometimes move beyond their reserve, whether a gesture of tenderness didn't bring them together, beyond all the crude sexual conjunctions. In other classes, husbands and wives, married by coercion,

2 Edward Shorter, op. cit., pp. 75 sqq.

66

learned to value each other, taking delight in getting to know one another. Their happiness and their sorrows were hardly different from our own, which makes these fellow humans, despite the distance, so close to us.

12

Restoring Reason to Sentiment

Just as a marriage for financial reasons can turn into a marriage for love, a marriage for love has to be coloured, if it wants to continue, by a certain amount of reason – provided that the compromises involved are chosen by the spouses and not imposed by their families. In other words, reason, expelled by sensibility, eventually returns as the latter's ally. Here we have to develop a conception of the intermediaries, transitions, and nuances: financial advantage can be coloured by a little affection, and affection can be coloured by calculation. Apart from the fact that financial marriages are not dead in the upper classes, and that swindlers and schemers always gravitate around wealthy old crones and ageing millionaires in order to extract money from them, to wring everything possible out of them, it is dangerous to ban money from the domain of love. Exiled from discourse, it reappears at the first bump in the road, and when it comes to divorce degenerates into a sordid settling of old scores. Then every moral or sentimental debt has to be paid in hard cash. To construct a couple solely on the basis of the heart is to build on sand. The all-devouring madness that connects two people at the beginning can be prolonged only if it is transformed into other, no less admirable bonds – closeness, sweet and trusting friendship. We have simultaneously to sublimate fervour and stir up cold-blooded cohabitation, multiply supports rather than reducing them to the hot breath of passion. To connect at any cost intensity with duration is to reject the passage of time and to expose ourselves to despair. In this sense 'good conjugal love' is a soft-spoken love that is taken for granted and allows spouses to go about their business without thinking about it, because they know they are enveloped in tender concern. It is a love that cares little for love, has nothing to prove, and spares itself the pathos of constant recruitment.

If adults go astray in the grip of their internal turmoil, that is no one's business but their own. Everything changes with the arrival of a child: he will remain the cement binding his parents even if they eventually separate. It is his need for continuity and protection that must be given priority. A promise not kept is always painful, but it becomes scandalous when it affects children (and all those fathers of the late 1960s who were so marvellously irresponsible know something about that). The solidity of a bond and the validity of a promise are best gauged at the height of a crisis. To fail to come through then is the greatest offence. The freedom we enjoy these days implies an increased responsibility. Once separated, parents must be able to get along well enough not to botch their divorce: they have to share the bringing up of their children, provide a safety net for them, and even manage the logistics of a blended family whose members may prove allergic to one another. (Blended families make one think of the collective apartments in the Soviet Union where, in the name of socialism, complete strangers had to live together in a small space. Today, in the name of attachment, we shoulder a heavier burden.) A successful separation is just as difficult to achieve as a successful marriage.

A formidable challenge: how can we reconcile the fleeting nature of the couple with the stability of its offspring? In the age of the pill, the condom, and abortion, having children is not unavoidable; their birth can be programmed, and we can no longer assign responsibility for them to nature. Thus impetuous lovers must be strongly urged to think twice before leaving a string of kids behind them as they pass from one infatuation to another, and to make full use of the means of contraception if they do not feel able to take responsibility for their children. A vagabond libido is perfectly legitimate so long as it does not lead to erratic procreation. We need laws to protect the weakest from the vagaries of the heart and to regulate attractions and repulsions. The child comes once and for ever, whereas love comes several times and for indeterminate lengths of time.

To rein in the anarchic dominance of the affects and to restore a degree of discernment to the cohabitation of men and women, we have to rehabilitate a traditionally scorned idea, that of fragmentation, or pursuing different aspects of one's life separately. This used to be reserved for husbands whose loves and desires were focused outside the household and who sought honours and approval in the offices they held; now it can be extended to everyone. 'Love is the whole life of a woman', Madame de Stael wrote in 1796, 'it is only one season in the lives of men'. This is no longer true: love is not the whole of life, there are activities that are just as vast, just as rich, and ambition can become an adventure for both sexes. Why should we burden ourselves with the yoke of marriage from the outset rather than embrace a more exciting destiny and delay making a commitment? Many women are just as concerned with their professional success as with their love lives, even if they have to avoid procreation or undertake it later on, making use of sophisticated scientific means. A fully developed emotional life is now compatible with a successful career (even if there are tensions between them; the whole objective of an intelligent family policy is to reconcile having children with work for women, and in this domain France is still a pioneer in Europe, because its birthrate is among the highest).

Thus we can dissociate the couple from the family, procreation from passion, and parenthood from marriage; we can live together and separately, have children alone without waiting for the perfect partner,[1] and return to the customs of the Old Regime, that is, accept a certain schizophrenia, compartmentalize our lives. Why not also imagine, alongside the new dating networks on the internet, the return of match-makers who would spare timid people the torments of seduction and could pair up the most dissimilar people? (In Denmark, a fishing village that has a serious lack of women 'imports' large numbers of wives from Thailand via the internet.) Rather than awkwardly trying to win the consent of a young beauty, why not allow a qualified person to negotiate on your behalf? In order to survive, marrying for love has to cross types and periods, make compromises with other, more traditional forms of nuptial union. Following the nineteenth-century utopian thinker Charles Fourier, the 1960s invented love relationships

1 In the United States, the term 'SWANS' (Strong Women Achievers No Spouse) is applied to mothers who have their children late and who conceive without being in a regular marriage, while the term 'SOD' (Start Over Dad) is applied to men who procreate after the age of sixty (quoted in Martine Segalen, 'Le mariage occidental à l'épreuve', in *Histoire du mariage*, op. cit., p. 1165.

that went beyond the bounds of the couple; today, we have to invent a couple that goes beyond the bounds of love and embraces experiences as varied as the understanding of the time: concern about the transmission of property, partnership, friendly tolerance, and mutual respect.

13

Together, Separated

'Love stories usually end badly.' Rita Mitsouko's famous song sounds good, but everything that ends is not bad in itself and the fact that a relationship comes to an end does not invalidate the grandeur or the beauty of its development. We need to maintain two contradictory propositions: on the one hand, life in a couple is not a marathon in which one has to hang on as long as possible, but rather a certain quality of bonds that one has to be able to break when they deteriorate. Brevity is no more a crime than endurance is a virtue: some fleeting affairs are masterpieces of concision that mark you for life, and some fifty-year-long relationships are foils for boredom and renunciation. But it is not dishonourable to prefer permanence to incandescence, as is shown by this remark made by a character in Christophe Honoré's film *Les Chansons d'amour* (2007): 'Love me less but love me longer.' A splendid formula: it is as if he senses that it is the very voraciousness of passion, its 'ebullient joy' (Montaigne), that kills life in common instead of nourishing it. The desire to grow old together is no less legitimate than the desire to burn in a spasm of the senses and the throes of emotion. We can want both freedom and a cocoon, we can want to enjoy both the warmth of the family hearth and the dizzying excitement of little interludes, we can fear loneliness more than weariness and put up with the matrimonial bond in spite of everything.

Pursuing the same line of thought, why not make eroticism optional, and have done with the imperative of sensual pleasure that is the folly of our time just as prudishness was that of earlier centuries? Consider the profundity of this witticism uttered by a close friend: 'I find it disgusting to sleep with those one loves.' Apart from the fact that love and sexuality are not always connected, why should the specifications of the couple be fulfilled to the letter without envisaging, for those who wish it, the possibility of a harmonious, celibate cohabitation? Paying homage to Venus is not imperative, and there is no need for torrid sessions and repeated embraces to value one another; Platonic relationships are not obsolete. Moreover, nothing forbids people from living together part-time, or having separate apartments (a supreme luxury), living separately in order to avoid confusing intimacies (with the associated pleasure of visiting one another), keeping a respectful distance, loving and desiring elsewhere – in short, from reviving the old aristocratic distinction between conjugality and affection: for an Old Regime noble, there was nothing more inappropriate than loving one's spouse.

Conjugal happiness is the art of the possible, and not the exaltation of the impossible; it is the pleasure of constructing a common world together. The couple can be adapted to numerous variations as soon as it is detached from the dream of a miraculous symbiosis that is supposed to enclose desires and aspirations. Like the nation in Renan's conception, it is also 'a daily plebiscite', a desire to avoid being eroded by the passing years, and a renewed trust and a renunciation of any irrational conduct: perpetual unpredictability, constantly putting in question what was settled yesterday, would be unbearable. In this domain as in others, the point is to define a new economy of the passions, resolutely to separate where one sought to bring together, and to combine where one sought to distinguish. The earlier binary system, in which people hesitated to put the rope around their necks, is slowly being replaced by today's hybrid system, in which we want everything and its contrary, to be both single and married, free and bound. Rites of passage have been irrevocably discredited: we now prefer the overlapping of ages, the interpenetration of ways of life. Marriage by consent or convenience, cohabitation, free unions, pacts of civil solidarity: this distribution is partly outdated; there are increasing numbers of intermittent spouses who live like single people and grant each other mutual freedoms, erotic friendships that mix genres, tranquil cohabitations in which the partners live like traditional spouses, and others that cannot be classified in any category, because they belong to all of them at once.

14

The Defeat of Prometheus

In 1904, on the occasion of the centenary of the French Civil Code, a commission was named by the Keeper of the Seals to bring it up to date. When the time came to consider proposition 212: 'Spouses owe each other mutual fidelity, aid, and assistance', the novelist and playwright Paul Hervieu asked for the floor:

I shall put forth a proposal that may seem subversive, and of whose audacity I am fully aware; however, I feel compelled to say what I think, and therefore I shall speak. The word 'love' is not used in the Civil Code: it is without any doubt the basis of marriage, the feeling that ennobles it. But the Civil Code is silent on this point. It seems to me that we have to indicate, by making room for this word, spouses' obligation to love one another.[1]

The proposal, which met with an enthusiastic response, was soon forgotten, and this legislative lapsus should be seen as a sign of wisdom. People can still get married without love being made obligatory, and perhaps some day it will be recommended that couples not love each other too much if they want to stay together over the long term. Marriage obviously will not disappear: even if it has become a kind of potluck to which everyone brings his own expectations and aspirations, it will remain, rightly or wrongly, a way of reducing uncertainty, an institutional rampart against the lurches of desire and the hazards of the affects. Perhaps the age at which people are allowed to marry should be raised to forty, the way retirement age is raised, in order to give future spouses ample time for reflection. Then, in an ironic reversal, marriage would no longer be a symbol of conformism, but instead a symbol of the elite, an adventure for a minor-

1 Quoted by Irène Théry in *Le Démariage*. Paris: Odile Jacob, 2001, pp. 77–8.

ity, a very exclusive club reserved for the happy few.

Since the Enlightenment our society has been haunted by a mad hope that the universal language of the heart, spreading from the private to the public sphere, will reconcile nations and raise the human family to the summits of harmony. This is a legend woven by poetry, in which Good defeats Evil through brotherhood and love. Once purged of its ugly sides, feeling would finally realize its divine essence: it would become a rose without thorns. 'Communism is love', a delegate to the Congress of Tours declared in 1920, during the foundation of the French Communist Party. Translation: anyone who is not a communist is consequently for hatred and no longer deserves to be counted as a human being. We recognize in this doctrine a secularized version of the Gospels; but Christianity took great care to defer the perfection of love to the afterlife, thus putting it beyond reach for mere humans – as if it sensed that, subjected to the flux of human becoming, this versatile king could only leave his worshipers distraught or furious. The condition of Pure Love is that it never occurs on Earth and remains an eschatological horizon. Our age of unbelief is saturated with Christian ideals that it embraces uncritically and dissimulates under the mask of disdain for religion.

Love has to be reinvented, Rimbaud wrote.[2] An unfortunate phrase, not that of a poet but of a planner, a CEO who wants to reconstruct something the better to subject it to his own views. In matters of feeling, the theory of progress is a theory of condemnation, because we have always to do better and because tomorrow will make today obsolete. We cannot rest on our laurels, we have to move forward; we are doomed, like Sisyphus, to eternal labour. However, love is not to be reinvented, but to be lived in all its tragic and magic dimensions simultaneously. It remains marvellous in that it cannot be reformed, just as happiness comes at the price of being accessible only in brief episodes. 'A civilization of love' (Benedict XVI) is no more desirable than the dream of goods free of charge in a mercantile economy: it would subject the weakest to the arbitrariness of the heart, to fleeting brotherhoods, to the secret reign of preferences. Feeling

2 'I don't like women. Love has to be reinvented' (*A Season in Hell*).

is a way of destroying human fellowship, because it creates the elect and the excluded. Similarly, everything that is given has to be paid for some day, in gratitude or even servitude. What we have to build is a society of decency and solidarity, not a society of charity.

The misadventures of marriage for love count among the illnesses of the murderous ideal, which are just as chimerical as Don Quixote's battles against the windmills, and attest to our difficulty in living together. Western cultures are caught in a vicious circle: we desire two things, happiness and love, that constantly escape our control, exactly as nature mocks, through its disturbances and eruptions, our will to dominate it. We pay a high price for having conflated passions and institutions. Our unreasonableness since the Enlightenment consists in the Promethean nature of our humours, our ambition to rule over the private and personal, even if only by tolerating it and making it into a generalized politics. Ultimately, societies can control emotions and bodies in two ways: by prohibiting them and by permitting them. One way prescribes, supervises, punishes; the other liberates, sets free, authorizes. Permission is subtler than prohibition, but the heart, with its complexity that foils all our plans and stubbornly resists the homage we do it, is still more subtle. We can build nothing without passion, but we cannot build anything durable on passion alone. To escape this antinomy, we have to rely on stable institutions that carry us through time and free us from the vacillations of subjectivity. Let us be glad, in a way, that our matrimonial utopias have collapsed: this proves that love retains its subversive power, that it remains the inconvenient demon who eats his own children by multiplying his demands. It is our attempt to tame love that has failed rather than marriage itself. Love is not, as we have said, a kind of glue whose adhesive power is supposed to be put in the service of the institution of marriage; it remains an explosive that blows up in our faces, dynamite pure and simple.

The Sweetness of Life

For the past half-century we have been pursuing, in the domain of manners and morals, a strange adventure: that of an emancipation that both liberates and oppresses us. Many taboos have fallen, but on their ruins new injunctions have proliferated. These injunctions are different in that they no longer prohibit but exhort and demand the maximum: we have to enjoy more, love more, earn more, consume more, speculate more, live more and without pause. In all these domains, a lack of moderation prevails over the logic of profit peculiar to the mercantile system. Everywhere, doctrinaire proponents of a standardized fever pitch are dominant. A strange misadventure for our generation, which is infatuated with the romantic and with justice, but is now noticing, rather late, that its revolutionary mottos – passion for life, intensity, and ecstasy – have become advertising slogans and hedonism has become the last stage of capitalism. (What needs to be invented today is a non-commercial hedonism that includes surprise, balance, and level-headedness, and that is first of all an art of living with others and not an art of self-enjoyment.) We are constantly called upon not to be satisfied with what we feel, to move beyond it. This immoderation attracts us but also destroys us, poisons our slightest joys, and leads us to engage in an insatiable quest. Presently, resisting these mirages must be our wisdom. A certain kind of unbridled liberation is self-contradictory in its principle, and creates the setting for its own defeat if it is not reined in by a sense of limits.

In ages of moral censorship, the right to caprice has to be defended, and in ages of permissiveness the principle of kindness. Since society has ceased to constrain us but persists in conditioning us, it is up to each individual to impose rules on himself. In this area, our best weapons are indulgence and delicacy: let us pardon each other our respective weaknesses, and avoid wounding those whom we cherish. Let us thank the people we love for existing, and for accepting us as we are.

That is what we call the sweetness of life.